There's a Bulldog on My Gas Tank

and Other Memories of WWII

by
Timothy Horner, OSB

There's a Bulldog on My Gas Tank

MathisJones Communications, LLC

Book Design by Ellie Jones
MathisJones Communications, LLC

Library of Congress Cataloguing-in-Publication data

ISBN# 978-0-9853093-1-2

Published by Monograph Publishing, LLC
1 Putt Lane
Eureka, Missouri 63025
636-938-1100

There's a Bulldog on My Gas Tank

and Other Memories of WWII

by
Timothy Horner, OSB

The reminiscences of any soldier of any war are unique. What happened to him may be surprisingly different even from what happened to the soldier next to him, and his reactions and memories will probably be still more different. In addition, the actual experiences of any soldier are far removed, for better as well as for worse, from the imaginings of those whom he has left at home, especially those who really care for him. This can be of some comfort to them.

For both these reasons reminiscences, however accurate, will be quite unlike the official history of the same war. That is partly why they can be so valuable.

War is a great evil. Much sorrow and many tragedies are caused by it, but one's life at war is not all about bullets and bombs, battalions and battleships. This is true even when one is in contact with the enemy, and anyway, one is not continuously in contact.

The versatile 25-pounder gun-howitzer, named for the weight of its shell, was for Britain the standard field artillery piece in WWII, and one of the best guns Britain ever produced. It had a team of six men.

Leading Up to the War

My first action that turned out to be connected with World War II, although I did not know so at the time, was to join the Artillery branch of the Reserve Officers Training Corps (ROTC) at Oxford University in 1938. War was possible then, but we did not think it would happen. I was persuaded to join by friends, who held before me the pleasure of riding through Oxford in the early morning on horseback. Unfortunately from that point of view, the artillery unit became mechanized and I never saw Oxford from a horse.

In the summer of 1939, I attended artillery camp and earned Certificate B. I already had Certificate A from the OTC at Ampleforth, the public (that is, private) school that I attended in England. Certificate A certified that I had reached a certain modest level of military skill. Certificate B raised the level and specified artillery skill. We were told at Ampleforth that Certificate A would assure us of a commission, should there be a war. Had that been true, there would have been almost as many officers as men in the army. At artillery camp, we were told the same about Certificate B, and that was more credible. On returning to Oxford, I was made an instructor in the ROTC for the following year, 1939-40, which stood me in good stead.

In mid-August, 1939, I drew from the bank a ten pound note nearly the size of a pocket handkerchief, and, with a friend from Oxford, set off on bicycle for a tour of Northern France. We sailed from Newhaven to Dieppe and spent the first night at the château of a champagne king, who was my friend's friend. As all our clothes for three weeks had to fit on the back of our bicycles, we could hardly dress for the occasion. At dinner, we found behind each chair a footman in long white gloves, who pushed our chair in under our shabby attire. Towards the climax of the meal, we were served the best champagne I have ever tasted, but when it came time for bed, we asked for a bath or shower. In the whole château there was only one bath, and this was the servants' night for it.

That was our only night of luxury. Thereafter we stayed in Auberges de Jeunesse (Youth Hostels), which were friendly and, rightly, economical. We were engrossed in the cathedrals and churches, which were our main objectives, with Chartres and its sculptures and stained glass outstanding, but with Beauvais and La Sainte Chapelle in close pursuit. We had no time to go to Laon. At Chartres, after a long bicycle ride on a hot day, we asked at our auberge for a bath or a shower. Neither was available, and they directed us to a water pump in the courtyard. Accordingly we stripped to the waist, found our soap and towels, and started to wash. Before long, the other youths were at their doors watching and wondering what ces fous Anglais (these mad Englishmen) were up to.

We enjoyed the Louvre and loved the Jeu de Paume, which in 1939 had all their Impressionist paintings hung in two rooms, which we preferred to their being scattered around the Musée d'Orsay as they are now. But we were not following the news. We went down to the appropriate railway station in Paris and enquired about tickets to Cologne, on the border with Germany. With a quizzical smile (ces fous Anglais again) the clerk said we should buy a newspaper not a ticket. We did so and saw that war was imminent. We jumped on our bicycles and headed for the North Coast. We spent a night in Beauvais, and next morning attended Mass at the Cathedral. The Bishop made an impassioned call for Faith in la Belle France, Hope that all would end well, Love for our gallant armed forces. His last sentence, incongruously, was 'And now let us pray for peace'. We reached Dieppe, bought a full-size bottle of Benedictine for less than 50 cents, and were just in time to catch one of the last ships from Dieppe back to Newhaven. We crossed the Channel early on September 1, 1939, the day that Hitler invaded Poland. I remember well that we were listening to Mozart's Oboe Concerto in my friend's home when we heard the news. I telephoned my mother, jumped on my bicycle and made for London

In Parliament, at 11:15 a.m. on September 3, 1939, Mr. Chamberlain, the British Prime Minister, declared war on Germany. At 11:30 a.m. all the air raid sirens went off, and we shuddered at this example of German efficiency, but it was nothing of the sort. Some careless civilian pilot had taken off on the East Coast without telling anyone.

Shortly after that I wrote to the appropriate authority and volunteered my services. I blush to add that I thought my most valuable contribution might be in the area of cryptography, but no doubt some wise old clerk in the War Office ignored my letter, and I was soon summoned before the Joint Universities Recruiting Board in Oxford. They were professors who had presumably served in World War I. Since then their brains and their bodies had expanded, but not their uniforms. They asked me what I sought, and I asked for a commission in the Artillery.

'Oh, Mr. Horner, are you reading Mathematics?'

'No.'

'When did you last study Mathematics?'

'My first year in high school.'

'But the artillery requires considerable skill in Mathematics. We think you would be far more suited for an infantry regiment.'

That was not at all what I wanted, and I nearly crept away in high dudgeon. But then I remembered that there was more to my case, and I added that I was a member of the Artillery ROTC.

'Oh, are you?'

'And I did attend Artillery camp this summer.'

'Oh, did you?'

'And I did get my Certificate B.'

'Oh, really?'

'And I should mention that I am an instructor in the ROTC.'

'Oh well, that does make a difference, doesn't it?'

So I was granted my request, and was told that I would hear from them in due course. I asked if they had any idea how due the course might be, and they replied sagely that this depended on the course of the war. I went back to Oxford, uncertain about my future. I did in fact have the whole academic year there.

There ensued the nine months of the 'phony war' when the Maginot and Siegfried lines confronted one another. In May, 1940, the Germans achieved what all assumed to be impossible, and passed a strong force through the 'impassable' Forest of the Ardennes. The collapse of France and the Allied escape through Dunkirk followed swiftly, and in England recruits were needed. But the facilities and matériel to train them were not immediately available and it was not until October 1940 that my turn came.

Before October I was, for some of the time, in London during air raids. I still remember the wailing sound of the air raid sirens, the noise of bombs falling and exploding, and the joyful, steady note of the 'all clear'. The morale of the civilian population was amazingly good. It was commonplace in the morning after a raid to see in the shattered glass of a shop window, a placard 'BUSINESS AS USUAL'. Even the damaging incendiary bombing of the business center of London caused anger rather than demoralization. Later the V 1 and V 2 rockets had more psychological effect.

Once there was a raid on a Saturday evening. Two bombs fell quite close to our house, but we heard no explosion. On Sunday morning we looked around and saw no damage, but on Monday morning there was pandemonium: air raid wardens' bells, police whistles, megaphones, etc. telling us to evacuate immediately. The UXB (Unexploded Bombs) Squad arrived to defuse and remove the bombs. When they had done so we were recalled, and we started to think. The bombs had fallen in the garden of a house where two dear old spinsters lived. We went round and congratulated them on being alive. We then asked when the bombs had fallen.

'Saturday night.'

'And when did you call the police?'

'Monday morning.'

'Wasn't that a bit of a risk?'

'Well, we couldn't disturb the dear police on a Sunday, could we?'

We thought they could, but did not say so.

Training and My First Regiment

During the long vacation from Oxford in the summer of 1940, I joined a friend who was organizing a group of older boys from the City of Oxford High School to go forestering in the Forest of Dean in south-west England. The coal mines needed pit props. The foresters cut down the trees, and we had to saw them into lengths varying with their diameter, and then stack the results. It was hard work, and in the evening we repaired to the local pub and regaled ourselves with draught cider. That west-country cider is stronger than beer. We were introduced to a dangerous game named Cardinal Puff. You took one gulp of cider, set the mug down once, tapped the table once with each forefinger, and then each side of your nose once. Then you raised yourself slightly from your chair and sat down again with one bump. That was the killer. On the next round you did everything twice and with two fingers and two bumps; and so on. There were penalties for mistakes, involving more cider. Not many of us ever reached a third round, and no one a fourth. Don't try it.

While we were forestering, France fell, and it was clear that those who had volunteered for service would be called up as soon as we could be trained. My turn came in October, but not before my mother and I in Kent in south-east England were able to watch the Battle of Britain in the sky above us. We did not recognize at the time how vital that battle was to us, and none of us knew that Göring had persuaded Hitler that he could with his Air Force bring Britain to her knees while Hitler dealt with France. Likewise, not many of us fully appreciated until much later how much we owed to the skill and courage of The Few in the Royal Air Force.

In October 1940, several of my Oxford friends and I were called to report to 121 Artillery OCTU (Officer Cadet Training Unit) at Alton Towers, Staffordshire, now a Butlin's Holiday Camp. It had a reputation as the most gentlemanly of the artillery OCTUs, but it was quite strict enough for us civilians. RTU (Returned To Unit) was the threat that hung ever over our heads, and nearly cut mine off on the first day.

Alton Towers was built in the nineteenth Century, roughly modeled on the old British castles. Its main feature was a magnificent Great Hall, with a fine open fireplace in the middle. Here we had our meals. We slept in scattered Nissen huts.

On our arrival, a Sergeant showed us around, pointed to some large sacks and a pile of straw and told us to fill a sack each. That was to be our mattress. We were given two blankets but no sheets. His last words to us were, 'There will be a test in Trigonometry first thing tomorrow morning.' After he had left, I asked George, one of my friends from Oxford,

'What is Trigonometry?'

'The measuring of Triangles.'

'Yes, the name says that; but how does it work?'

'Can you read logarithm tables?'

'Yes.'

'Have you heard of SOHCAHTOA?'

'No. What does it mean?'

'Sin = Opposite over Hypotenuse; Cosine = Adjacent over

Hypotenuse; Tan = Opposite over Adjacent.' It applies only to right-angle triangles. There are two other rules: A over Sin A = B over Sin B = C over Sin C; and . . .'

At that point I stopped him and said I would stick with SOH-CAHTOA and hope there would be enough right-angle triangles. There were; I aced those and flunked the rest, earning just enough marks not to be RTU.

There was a certain amount of plain drill, during which I learnt that one of our sergeant's favorite phrases was 'The bigger they are, the dafter they are'. There was more gun drill with field artillery guns, which we never fired. They taught us to drive a vehicle, since it was not unusual then for a young man of twenty not to know how to drive.

It was a severe winter with snow and ice: one of our men left our truck hanging partly over a precipice. We had to get out carefully on the other side. The only driver who hit another vehicle was our instructor. We learnt that army accident reports usually started 'I was driving at 15 mph on my own side of the road when , . . . '

On Sundays in England we were divided into C. of E., R.C., or O.D., that is, Church of England, Roman Catholic, or Other Denominations, and were marched off to the appropriate church. The alternative to Church Parade was burdensome fatigue duty, so religious attendance was almost 100%. The Catholics were taken to Mass by truck to Cheadle to what many think is Pugin's most beautiful chapel.

Besides drill, we had many classes and lectures on guns, radio, vehicles, tactics, and so on. A Cavalry Officer came to address us. The Cavalry had the reputation of being the most elegantly turned out part of the army, and the least brainy. The old joke said of them that there was once a Cavalry Officer who was so brainless that his fellow officers noticed.

Our Cavalry Officer, whose regiment had recently been converted from horses to tanks, started in that curious, dry, back of the throat, army voice, 'My topic this morning, gentlemen, is Tank-proof Localities. A tank-proof locality, gentlemen, is a locality proof against tanks.' Logically sound, but I heard no more. I was also the only one who giggled, but no one noticed. I was reminded of our weapons instructor at Ampleforth, Sergeant Huggan, who was dear to all of us, and who knew the army pamphlet on weapons by heart. He was instructing us on how, when firing a rifle, to aim off for wind. 'First estimate the wind speed, then double it, and then . . .' When he had finished, he turned to one of us and asked how to aim off for wind. The cadet answered that you estimate the wind speed, multiply it by two . . .

'No, Sir.'

'But, Sergeant, that's exactly what you said: you estimate the wind speed and then multiply it by two, you double it.'

'That's right, Sir, you double it.'

One evening in the Great Hall of Alton Towers we were to hear one of Prime Minister Churchill's radio addresses to the country. By chance there was a power-cut that evening, and we listened by the flickering light from the great fireplace, a most dramatic setting. I think it was the speech that included the plea to the United States, not yet at war, 'Give us the tools and we'll finish the job'. I was reminded of this a year or two later when we were joined by a Division that was not mechanically adept. The exhortation was changed to 'Give us the job, and we'll finish the tools'.

Quite recently I read in a historical journal a debunking article claiming that Mr. Churchill never changed anything. But he did: he changed the spirit of a nation, not least by 'marshalling the English language and sending it into battle'.

Our colonel had a pack of beagles. There was a pack at Ampleforth, with which I had run on occasion, so I was somewhat acquainted with the habits of hares, the most relevant being that they tend to run in a circle. I was out beagling at the OCTU. It was raining, and I was running beside the Colonel along a slippery, rutted, farm track. I slipped and barged into him. I apologized, asked if he was all right, and ran on. It may have been my most significant action at the OCTU, as my final report read in toto:'This well-mannered cadet should make a good officer.' There was nothing about gun-drill or other such technicalities.

In May 1941, after a few days leave, I joined 136 (First West Lancashire) Field Regiment of the Royal Artillery, part of the 55th Division, on the South Coast of England. By day, it was a gentle form of army life: parades, including church parade, inspections, maintenance of equipment, etc. The rigor came at night.

Our task was to help protect the coast from German invasion and, as the German barges were visible from the air on the far side of the English Channel, such an invasion was for all that summer quite probable. It was one of Hitler's great mistakes that he failed to take advantage after Dunkirk of our shortage of manpower and especially of matériel, and went after a paralyzed France rather than a severely depleted England. It was well for our regiment and an answer to prayer that he did so, since we were the very first line of defense.

We had twenty-four guns to fire onto the beaches of the landing areas. But there were high cliffs there. Only eight of our guns could have done what was needed. The second eight were beautiful guns, French 75s, but their muzzle velocity was so high that their shells, if they were to clear the cliffs, would have landed far out to sea. The last eight were the right type of gun, or more accurately howitzer, but were made in the nineteenth century and had stamped on the breech block FOR DRILL PURPOSES ONLY: NOT TO BE FIRED. We took these eight out onto the South Downs and fired a round of gunfire, but we never even saw where some of the shells landed.

The invasion was most likely to come by night or at dawn. On the coast, left over from the Napoleonic invasion-scare, was a Martello Tower in surprisingly good condition over a hundred years later. We occupied it by night, and from it we kept watch. The door was about twenty feet up, reached by a ladder, which was taken away after we entered, and brought back next morning. There were two floors, the upper for watching, the lower for resting. There was a fireplace on the lower floor. One night sparks from it set part of the floor on fire. Our watch put it out with difficulty. Had they failed, we would have had a twenty-foot jump down onto the rocks. After that we were equipped with a long rope and buckets of sand, and we hauled the ladder up inside the Martello Tower. There was one scare when the watch at first light saw some ships close in shore. The watch raised the alarm, but the ships were a group of friendly merchantmen seeking overnight shelter from a storm. I am glad I was not on duty that night.

In my troop one of the few Catholics was Gunner Pershouse. One evening the phone rang and Eastbourne Jail wanted to know if we had a Gunner Pershouse. I said Yes. (Now, the army has a regulation that in case of dire emergency a driver may urinate against the nearside rear wheel of his vehicle. Pershouse had chosen the wrong wheel and the military police escorted him to jail). Would someone come and fetch him? When I arrived, they asked me whether he was a good citizen and well behaved. I vouched for him. As we approached his cell, a prisoner was singing at the top of his voice, 'I am a bloody Catholic: I love my bloody Faith'. This was Pershouse. The sentiments were creditable even though their expression was not, so I took him home.

Another evening, the phone rang, and this was much more serious. Again it was about Pershouse. He was driving on a roller-coaster path along the edge of the cliffs and had parked on a down slope and put the brakes on. The brakes failed and the truck rolled down its slope and partly up the other side, where it hit a rock and fell over into the sea. Next day we assembled a jib, pulley, tackle, acetylene torch and a cylinder of compressed air and set off to recover the vehicle. The only way down to the sea was through a minefield. Luckily there was also a light railway track through the minefield, which we followed and reached the vehicle safely. It was not too difficult to cut the vehicle into three parts and haul those by the pulley to the top of the cliff. That left us at the bottom, but by then the tide had come in and cut us off. Our only way to the top was by the pulley. The cylinder of compressed air went next, safely, to my relief; then we too followed safely, but inelegantly, as none of us had heard of rappelling. That was my moment of greatest danger so far.

From South Coast to Simon

The South Coast held other attractions for me. One came through our Commander, Royal Artillery (CRA) the head artilleryman of the Division. He had a bad start with us. In his first address to all his artillery officers he stressed more than once that each of us was personally responsible for his vehicle. If our vehicle would not start, it was our fault. He then walked to his vehicle in front of all of us, and it would not start. But he was a keen cricketer and, in my eyes at least, he more than redeemed himself by arranging a cricket tournament for the artillery regiments of the Division. Our regiment won this. The Artillery then challenged the rest of the Division and won. Our Division was then asked to play against another team in a charity match for some good cause. That match ended in a draw. Both teams included some Test Match and County players, the equivalent of all star and major league baseball players, and I was lucky to be included in our eleven. In the second over, I dropped a catch from their Test player, later had him dropped off my bowling, and finally caught him on the boundary by the sight screen just after he had made his century. We had no more cricket until after the war.

Late in the autumn, the Top Brass decided that the weather was too bad for an invasion, and we were sent north for the winter to Scrayingham, a village about fifteen miles north-east of York. It does not rate even a mention in the Blue Guide; we would concur. By that time I had been put in charge of all the vehicles in our battery. I spent much of my time inspecting them, which meant lying under them and testing prop shafts and other such bits of metal with my bare hands. It was an especially cold winter and I had no gloves.

But there was light relief even in that. We were due to be inspected by the Chief of the Imperial General Staff, Sir John Dill. He was the top soldier in England. There was much cleaning, polishing, and repainting. The last included repainting all the numbers on each vehicle. Our sign-writer, Gunner Jupp, repainted a light truck, of which the number was Z 4181425. Late in the day before the inspection, I inspected our vehicles and saw that the number on this truck was back to front, 5241814 Z. In a mixture of panic and fury I summoned Jupp and dressed him down, ending with 'how on earth did you manage to do this?' He totally defused my feelings by replying in pleasant West-country speech, 'Well, Zur, the trook moost 'ave bin facin' th' wrong way'. How could one be angry after that?

Three other little incidents involved motor-cycles (MCs), on which I had by then had much practice. I propped up my machine by the roadside and went to deliver a message. By the time I came back, it had fallen over and a small amount of petrol had escaped from the carburator. When I tried to start the MC, the spark ignited the petrol, which caught fire but did not explode. By now I owned a pair of heavy gloves and was able to beat it out with my hands.

Another time we were coming home up the Great North Road after a grand exercise in the Midlands. There had been several inches of snow, which the many heavy lorries had pressed down into an icy surface. 30 mph was the maximum speed for safety. We were in convoy but I on my MC had to get forward from the back of the column. I was going more than 30 mph and skidded. I was wearing my army great coat and a helmet. I spun around once or twice, but was able to get up and go on. Soon after that they decided that all MCs should be put into trucks. Either incident could easily have resulted in a notice, 'Died on active service'. It made me wonder how many such notices referred to such accidents. But this cloud, too, had a silver lining. The quad (Gun Tractor Vehicle) that I got into had a leaky radiator. We stopped at a house in Doncaster to get some water for it. When they brought it, they invited us to tea, a real Yorkshire tea with roast beef and Yorkshire pudding. There were five of us, and they would accept no payment until I suggested they could buy some toys for their children.

The third incident was much happier. One of my fellow officers had a British bulldog called Simon. Simon and I became good friends, and then his owner was posted to another formation. I was riding my MC along a very narrow street in York with stop-start traffic, when I saw Simon in the back of a truck two or three vehicles ahead of me. Without thinking I yelled 'Simon', and he jumped out of the back of his truck, came lickety-split down the sidewalk, jumped onto the MC's large gas tank between me and the handlebars, and started licking my face. His own driver had not noticed Simon's absence when the traffic started to move, and here was I stranded with a bulldog on my gas tank. I hooted in vain. Then I shouted as loud as I could 'There's a bulldog on my gas tank' and the traffic stopped. Simon was put back where he should have been. That was fun, and not a life-threatening moment.

The modern bulldog is, despite its look, friendly and gentle. The picture shows a female, but Simon looked much the same. Simon was gentle unless you tried to enter his master's room in his master's absence.

We Are Sent Abroad

When the weather became calm enough again for an invasion, we returned to the South Coast for the summer, and then north again for the next winter. We held manoeuvres in the South of Scotland. One night we camped at a farm near Kirkcudbright, and I had a stall next to a very handsome bull. In the middle of the night he started moving around and pressing on the flimsy partition and snorting a bit. But it passed, and I lived to scratch his head in farewell next morning. That could have been life-threatening, but was not. I had better luck with animals than with things.

That winter I was sent on a six-week signaling course. We had to learn about field-telephones and their maintenance, wireless sets and their maintenance, electricity and magnetism, and so on. My happiest memory is of watching a number of recruits learning to drive 3-ton lorries. Ten or so of them were lined up and started their engines. On the signal to go, they must all have let in their clutch with a bang. All ten lorries hopped forward almost in time with one another, until they gathered speed and calmed down. I received a D for the course and was a bit startled until I found out that it stood for Distinguished. I am grateful that the army filled in these and many other gaps in my scientific knowledge. It was probably because I had those gaps that I had to work harder at the courses.

When I returned to my regiment, I was put in charge of all the Battery's signalers and their equipment and was told to teach them how to use and maintain them. That was almost my first experience at the blackboard end of a classroom. I was lucky to have students who knew that their lives might depend on mastering what I was teaching. They were attentive and reached a high level of theoretical competence. We then went out on a practical exercise, and there was chaos. We still had to bridge the gap between theory and practice, but in the end, they turned out very well.

During our second northern sojourn, rumors started that we would soon be sent abroad. The orders came. We sent off our guns ahead of us and prepared for the move, but when the guns had gone, our move was cancelled. Just as well: our guns reached Singapore in time to be captured by the Japanese. We received new guns, and soon, we ourselves were ordered to move, and really did move. We embarked at Liverpool on January 14, 1943 in HMS Mooltan, a liner of the P. and O. line, converted to 'merchant cruiser' by the addition of two elderly six-inch guns in the stern and several good Oerlikon anti-aircraft guns amidships. She was 660 feet long with a complement of 700 or so. There were 4900 on board, with lifeboats, lifebelts, etc. for perhaps half of us.

A few days out we ran into a North Atlantic storm, not perhaps a 'perfect storm' but not far short of that. Even the regular seamen were impressed. There were four officers in each single berth cabin, which was a crowd, but spacious compared with the troops below deck. Few officers and fewer troops escaped seasickness. I was one of the lucky ones.

During the storm I was on the top deck and saw, when we were in the trough of the waves, water above me all the way round. That night I was on duty and walking thoughtlessly on the windward side, when a mighty wave came sweeping over our bow. It knocked me off my feet and rolled me towards the side of the ship. There were rails where I reached the side, otherwise I would have been overboard and the convoy would not have known. After the wave passed, I fled to the leeward side. Again my Army greatcoat protected me and kept out most of the water, so I was in surprisingly good shape. That was certainly life-threatening.

But when I looked around on the leeward side, I got another shock: the ship next to us in the convoy was heading straight towards us. We had been ordered not to go up to the bridge, so at first I did not. I thought the men on the bridge must have seen the other ship; but then I also thought that if by chance they had not, and if there were to be a collision, and if I were still alive, it would be hard to live with. So I approached the bridge and, as nonchalantly as I could, mentioned the other ship. 'Oh yes' they replied, 'her steering-gear broke earlier in the storm. Don't worry. They are trying to repair it.' The storm lasted several days.

My next mishap was only embarrassing. All the officers ate in one of the ship's main dining rooms. After the meals, the Colonel, his Second-in-Command, his Adjutant, and a senior Battery Commander liked to play bridge. One evening one of them was absent. I happened to pass by their table; they asked if I played bridge and, without thinking, I said I did. 'Come and join us.' 'Yes, Sir.' I was neither an expert player nor particularly keen. The man on my left opened with 'one spade', which, with all the surrounding noise, I did not hear. My partner followed with two hearts which, having not heard the opening bid, I I took to be a forcing two, indicating a strong hand and a fistful of hearts. I had a decent hand, so we soon got to a little slam, doubled and redoubled. When my partner put down a very ordinary hand, I knew we were in trouble. We went six down. My excuse was not accepted. As soon as we finished the rubber I escaped, and they made no attempt to stop me. I was never asked again, nor would I ever have accepted.

There were bright spots too. I learnt how to use a heliograph, which, with the help of the sun, can send a visual signal a long way, the record being 183 miles. From a course on unarmed combat I learnt three lethal blows, how to shake hands and break a man's shoulder, and how to disarm a man who attacks you with a knife. I have never used any of them, though as a schoolmaster I have been tempted. We also saw the Southern Cross in the evenings. I was doubtful about a few stars being able to be beautiful and moving, but they were, and not only to Christians.

In the South Atlantic we circled for a whole day to avoid U-boats. We passed Capetown with Table Mountain on one side and spouting whales on the other. At Durban we had our only shore leave. We went into a hotel and saw a huge bowl of fruit on each table. We assumed, after British rationing, that they were of wax; but they were real, and so good. We took a train inland towards Pietermaritzburg. It was a long train, and on one tight curve we saw our tail coach going in the opposite direction to our own coach. We left Durban sadly, escorted by the patriotic and nostalgic singing of 'The Lady in White', Mrs. Gibson.

Training in India for the Jungle

We reached Bombay without further adventure, and went thence by train to Ahmednagar, a regular military cantonment, where our training in Indian ways began. There we met two species of poisonous snakes, Cobra and Krait; we learnt that scorpions like to shelter in footwear, so it was wise to tap the heel on the ground before putting on the boot. That became a habit so ingrained that I found myself still doing it years after the end of the war. At our first meal, the kitchen was in one building and the dining hall in another. As we crossed the intervening space kites swooped down and grabbed whatever was on our plates. Despite their four-foot wingspan those birds could clean the plate without touching you.

Mosquitoes were the chief menace. We were told many times never to sleep without a mosquito net; always, if even one mosquito got inside your net, to kill it before going to sleep; always to take the Mepacrin or Quinacrin. We were also inoculated against various diseases. It was good to be at the head of the line as needles were scarce and each had to be used many times. Although sterilized between jabs, they did get blunt, and the line might be fifty men.

We also met the char-wallahs, or tea-men. The tea was hot, strong, and sweet. The char-wallahs walked around the cantonment, each carrying on his back a huge cylinder of hot tea, a good thing to drink in hot weather. It keeps the perspiration going and so protects against the heat. This was a gentle acclimation to India, and was welcome, but we were not able to do much training as we had no guns.

We next moved by train to Narsingpur in the middle of India. Here we did meet our guns. We also joined an Indian Army formation, the 7th Indian Division, known unofficially as the Pope's Own Division because the General, the CRA (Commander, Royal Artillery), the AQMG (Assistant Quarter-Master General), and others were Catholic. Our CRA came to inspect his new regiment, met each officer and asked where he had been at school and college. I duly said that I had been at Ampleforth and Christ Church, at which he showed no emotion. But when he returned to his headquarters, he summoned his Brigade Major,

Lionel (Bulgy) Leach, who had also been at Ampleforth and Christ Church, and told him about me. Sight unseen, Bulgy said that I must join their headquarters. And so, in a few weeks, it happened. I was promoted to Captain and received more pay. I was glad about that and also about leaving my Battery Commander, who was one of two men that I really disliked in my six years in the army. I must add, however, that he gave me one of the best bits of advice I have ever received: 'Never be rude on paper. If you must be rude, let it be face to face.'

At Narsingpur we could at first, having no trucks, move about only on foot in country which supported tigers, elephants, bears, wild pigs, snakes, and mongooses, Kipling country in fact. We finally met our guns and started training for the jungle, but we still could not do much because in the full heat of the sun the guns were too hot to handle.

When I reached my new job at HQRA (artillery headquarters), I had to get used to dealing with telephones and paper rather than with men and guns. I also had to get used to dealing constantly with a Brigadier and other officers far senior to me. That went well, and several of us remained friends for life.

A few weeks later we moved by train to Ranchi, some 200 miles west of Calcutta. Those long train journeys were quite leisurely. Before each meal an orderly came round with a menu and took our orders, which were telegraphed ahead to the next stop, where we left the train and went to our meal. As soon as the train stopped, the troops made a dash for the engine (steam) to get hot water for tea. Some trains were only for the army; others carried civilians too, who had their own coaches with every inch occupied and with some passengers and baggage on the roof. At one station we saw many passengers squatting on the platform with the whole soles of their feet flat on the ground, a position few westerners can hold for long. Their train was not due until the following day.

At Ranchi, we continued our training. Each morning we rose at 6 a.m. and the sun rose with us. The temperature might be delightfully in the 70s. Each day we hoped it would stay so, but it always rose into the 90s. Here we had our first taste of the monsoon. We were told to dig a trench 18 inches wide and 18 inches deep all round each tent. Those who disbelieved were flooded out almost at once, and any equipment on the ground was spoiled. I have never experienced so heavy a downpour lasting for so long.

My happiest memory from Ranchi is of attending Mass in a fine church with only a dirt floor. The pastor was an elderly, bearded, Belgian Jesuit. There were no pews, but they put out chairs at the front for the five sahibs, who were the only Westerners there. The men stood on one side, the women on the other, and sang a litany all through the Mass. It was distracting at first, but I gradually came to find it peaceful and meditative. The only word I caught was Swami (Lord). They were not singing in Urdu. Our Division had a Catholic chaplain, but he was invalided out fairly soon after we reached the Arakan and I do not remember his being replaced until much later.

It was at Ranchi, as Mess Secretary for the artillery headquarters, that I first thought about our diet. Curry was frequent. New to me were mangoes and lichees, both delicious. I have not had their like anywhere else. The curry varied with the place. In the cooler north of India the curry was milder, but the farther south you went, the hotter the weather and, surprisingly, the hotter the curry. We were also introduced to the chagal, a gray canvas bag which we filled with water and carried exposed to the sun, usually on the outside of our jeep. Then, by what the army called 'refrigeration by evaporation', when we had recourse to this dirty, dust-covered object, we had a long drink of ached-for cold water.

In Ranchi, too, I learnt a lesson in communication. One evening, I needed some hot water for my canvas bath, three feet square and a few inches deep. I rehearsed in my mind the necessary Urdu sentence, stopped an Indian soldier and, with all my grammar and syntax said haltingly to him 'Er, bhistiko . . . bolo . . . ke sahibko . . . kuchh garam . . . pani chahiye . . . guslkewasti'

(Tell . . . water-carrier. . . sahib needs . . . some hot water . . . for bath). He looked blank, so I said it again, and again. Eventually a British soldier who had been in India for years came by and asked what the trouble was. I explained, and he said to the Indian, 'Bolo the Bhisti to pakaro some pani jeldi' (Tell water-carrier bring water quickly) His grammar and syntax were minimal but he uttered the key words with conviction, and the Indian understood. The Indian said, 'Thik hai' (OK), and the water came. Conviction and self-confidence trumped grammar and syntax.

To the Arakan and Into Battle

When orders came for our move to the Arakan in north-west Burma, we discovered that there was, on the War Establishment for HQRA, no place for an Assistant Staff Captain, so I was sent to Divisional Headquarters as a Liaison Officer on the Operations Staff, somewhere between an office boy and an ADC, but much closer to office boy. There is much to be said for starting at the bottom.

We went by train to Madras, low down the East Coast of India, then by ship at night, because of Japanese air raids, back across the Bay of Bengal up to Chittagong in the southern part of what is now Bangladesh, a crazy itinerary made necessary by the transport available and the nature of the terrain. It was a bit like going from New Orleans to Mexico and back to Tallahassee.

From Chittagong we went by road south into the northern tip of the Arakan, with a pleasant two-day stop at a seaside camp en route. We swam in the sea, where one of our men was stung by a jellyfish and was sick for several days.

Finally we reached what was to be our battle area for the next seven months. We were to operate in Central Burma, having the Americans to our north, round the Burma Road to China. The morale of the troops we relieved was low. Since the fall of Singapore in February 1942 – and it was now August 1943 – the allied troops had been retreating slowly up the Malay Peninsula, through part of Thailand, and on up through Burma. This is about 1600 miles as the crow flies, and much more as the infantryman marches. The Japanese were in pursuit and had in one area entered India. It was our job to stop them and to drive them back.

Our first weapon was psychological: a visit from our Supreme Allied Commander, Lord Louis Mountbatten and his wife, Edwina. The message announcing his coming stressed that there should be minimum preparations, 'just a couple of oil drums to stand on'. I had to make the preparations, and gave him just that. He seemed a bit miffed, but he jumped up on them and gave a great speech. His best line was, 'If you have any needs, just let me know, and I'll send a telegram to my cousin the King, and we'll fix it.' We all knew well that the King could not fix things like that, but we loved the panache. He was not so gripping as Mr. Churchill, but he did have a real effect on morale, So, later, did General Slim.

We had other visitors too: Dame Vera Lynn, 'the forces' sweetheart', came and sang to us. No other entertainer came so close – a mile or two -- to the front line. There were also two VIPs from New Delhi. I was to meet them on the north bank of a medium sized river, bring them across it and then to our headquarters. I asked the Royal Engineers for a motor-boat. They assured me there were none, so I procured two sampans. A sampan is an oversized canoe propelled by one oar in the stern. In my innocence I thought the VIPs might enjoy the adventure and admire the skill of the boatmen. They did not; and to make matters worse, the one motor-boat on the whole river crossed our bows when we were half-way across.

Low mountain ridges divided the land into valleys running north and south. These ridges, a kind of curling tail to the Himalayas, were covered with dense jungle. Between the ridges, which were several miles apart, there was usually a river and open paddy fields of rice. We started in the westernmost valley but were due to move into its eastern neighbor, the valley of the Kalapanzin River. The only connection at first was a narrow path over the Goppe Pass, possible only for men and mules. Our chief Medical Officer was a Pathan from Pakistan and a full Colonel. He prided himself on being a great walker, and set his record for the crossing. I was sent across the pass on duty and decided to try to break his record. He was much older than I, and I succeeded. He was also much senior to me, so I never told him.

One sad incident: the colonel of my old regiment, whom I admired, had been in India twice or more, had suffered most of the Indian diseases, had been told by his doctors never to go back, but did come back with us. It was too much for him. One night, within easy range of the Japanese, he lit a cheroot, stood on the top of his slit trench and waved the cheroot at the Japanese and, with derogatory comments, urged them to shoot at him, which they did. He was invalided out and sent back to Ireland.

Shortly after that we were ordered across the Mayu Yoma and into the Kalapanzin Valley, in which there were no petrol (gas) engines except those needed for charging the radios. We traveled by foot, on horseback, or by sampan; equipment went on mules. It was war in slow motion. The approach to our new Headquarters was along a path one elephant wide. We soon came to a pile of elephant droppings nearly a foot high and still warm. It was in the middle of the path. We hoped the elephant would keep going. When we had to leave the path, we hacked our way with machetes through dense, virgin jungle at the rate of about 200 yards an hour. We were probably the first white men, possibly the first humans, to set foot there.

Our site was on a hillside, so we had to level spaces for our offices, to be covered by tarpaulins rather than tents. We made tables and chairs from the abundant bamboo. One of our Gurkha orderlies was so adept at this with his kukri that we christened him Mez banao (make table).

Despite the heat, we wore Battle Dress all the time in the jungle, because wherever we went, we encountered ticks very much like American ticks, and leeches about an inch or two long. The leeches lived on the branches and if they heard us coming, raced down to the end of their branch to greet us. If we pulled them off our body, they, like the ticks, might leave their heads in us to turn septic. We burnt them, or covered them with butter or ghi so that they could not breathe. There were also much longer leeches that lived in streams, so swimming was risky. A large leech entered my friend, Major Leach, who became known as Major Leech-Leach, or 'the hyphenated major'. Mosquitoes were present in plenty and the same stringent rules about taking Mepacrin applied as in India. An African division on our flank picked up a rumor that Mepacrin affected their virility. They refused to take it, so we had to start a counter rumor that it was an aphrodisiac. Then they wanted double.

Life at Divisional Headquarters was quiet. We were still in the monsoon and the ground was too soggy for anything except patrolling, and the weather often too bad for much activity in the air. I went on various errands over rough ground and mostly on horseback, which I enjoyed. I was promoted from Liaison Officer to General Staff Officer Grade 3 (the lowest) for Chemical Warfare (GSO 111, CW). Gas was in fact never used in Burma, though we had one scare, so in effect I was just one of the operations staff.

One notable member of the headquarters was our Afghan cook, Dhost Mahommed. Like Cleopatra, he used henna to dye his hair, and, unlike her, his beard, a light reddish-brown. An attractive rogue. Give him a good kitchen and plenty of supplies and he would produce an ordinary meal. But let there be thunder and rain, no shelter and not much food, and he would go off into the jungle, find jungle chicken and a variety of foods, and produce a banquet.

Both sides were planning a major offensive to start as soon as the monsoon ended. Ours was for February 6, 1944, but the Japanese got in first on the night of February 4/5. We awoke early in the morning of February 5 to be told that we had Japanese in front of us, on one flank, and in our rear. The other side was a mountain range. We dressed hastily, destroyed as many files as we could, and went out by the back way towards the mountain, leaving almost everything behind. . During a vigorous clamber, we were shot at, and the bullets coming through bamboo made a noise unlike anything I had ever heard. I did not even recognize it as bullets. We dropped to the ground. There were no more shots, so we went on and came down into a chaung (stream) along which we waded until we reached an area which came to be called the Administrative Box. It was a little more than a mile square. In it were stored supplies of all kinds: food, ammunition, medicine, clothing etc. We did not know whether the Japanese had reached it first, so I climbed up the bank of the chaung to see. I was wearing not boots but rubber-soled shoes, which slipped on the bank. Someone in boots passed me and reported that all was clear, and I was left looking stupid and cowardly. The latter at least was untrue.

By that time, the Engineers had converted the track over the Ngakyedauk Pass, known to the troops as the Okeydoke, into a lane passable for tanks, quite a feat. It ended in the Administrative Box. One troop of tanks had come over it and became invaluable.

We found that, besides the supply staff, who were not frontline soldiers, there was in the Box roughly a Brigade, that is three battalions of infantry and their service units, plus the four tanks. We hurriedly set up a rudimentary headquarters. Our first job was to make radio contact with the other two brigades of our division, to tell them where we were and how we were. They had each formed their own boxes and were well dug in. While we were establishing communication, we too were digging in. My orderly and I had a two-man slit trench overlooking a chaung thirty to fifty yards away, which by that night became part of the boundary between us and the Japanese, though they had not reached there while we were digging. So, not for the last time, Divisional Headquarters was part of the front line.

The Japanese quickly surrounded us and waited for us to surrender, as all previous allied formations had been forced to do. But our Army Commander had long foreseen this possibility and had developed a new plan. He had airstrips built within reach of the front lines, and ample supplies dumped there, so that any formation in our unfortunate position could be supplied by air. And so, after a day or two, we had constant supplies of food, ammunition, medicines, clothing, and even mail flown in for us, through mountainous country and often through dangerous weather. The majority of the pilots and planes were American, the rest British, and to them we owe our survival. We had general command of the air, but on our first day in the Box, a plane looking like a Hurricane appeared. I was standing by a path. It was only when I saw coming towards me on the path little spurts of dust that I realized that it was firing at me. I took cover, and the only casualty was one mule wounded, which I had to dispatch.

That first night was hair-raising. An account written later by a veteran describes it thus:

"The opening attack was an eruption of unbridled violence so intense that my mind could barely cope. Curtains of tracer bullets poured out of the darkness from seemingly every angle, mortar bombs rained down and the earth shook with the explosions of screaming shells. Blinding phosphorous bombs lit up the night, setting ablaze the bush around us. The world seemed to have gone mad amid a fury of flashing lights. . . . Most harrowing of all was our total inability to see our attackers." (Northern Daily Mail 23 June 2001).

He does not add that it was reported that the Japanese had bullets that made the usual explosion when they left the rifle and then a second explosion at the end of their course, so each bullet sounded as if it came from two directions; nor does he mention a most nerve-wracking enemy tactic: in the darkness a voice speaking good English, perhaps a prisoner under duress, would call out 'Sergeant Smith, Sergeant Smith, come and help me, I'm wounded.' We had to assume that the aim was to make us reveal our positions, but we could never be completely sure that it was not a genuinely wounded man.

Astonishingly, they did not attack that night while we were still unorganized. Presumably they thought we were bound to surrender. They did not know how many or where we were, any more than we knew how many or where they were. My orderly and I watched from our slit trench in turns, but not even at first light was there any attack.

We survived the night. Next morning we had time to take in our surroundings. On one side were the mountains of the Mayu Yoma. Dotted around on the other sides were hillocks, which we occupied. The Japanese attacked and we counter-attacked, but by and large we were able to maintain possession of them. The enemy did establish an observation post on a peak of the mountains, and our Air Force sent dive-bombers to deal with it. We had a great view of their vertical dive and their flattening out.

We thought the Japanese had only one field gun, probably 105 mm (4.1 inches) and not much ammunition. They fired only at dusk and dawn. One shell landed not too far from me as I was walking past a row of large oil drums. I thought I heard shell-splinters striking the drums both ahead of and behind me. I also thought that to run would be bad for morale, but I soon learnt better. You cannot be brave against a shell. It was an odd feeling to walk around, not knowing whether and when you would be shot at.

Part of the daily routine was the General's evening broadcast to his other two Brigadiers in their Boxes. There was much static in the jungle in the evenings. My voice was thought to come through it well, so I did much of the broadcasting. The wireless set was in a bren-carrier, a small, open, tracked vehicle with half-inch steel sides and floor. One evening I was on the air and heard a very loud explosion in my headphones. When I had finished, I asked what had happened and was told that a small shell had exploded under the bren-carrier. There were two or three of us in the carrier, and we must be among only a few who were a foot or two from an exploding shell, however small, and emerged unharmed.

Another evening one of the nightly Japanese shells landed in the area where all our reserves of ammunition were stacked. This caused some of the stacked ammunition to exlode. The officer who succeeded me at Artillery headquarters went to see if he could check the damage and was succeeding until fragments from one of the explosions broke his leg. I could easily have been in his place, but God had other plans.

One night the Japanese raided our Main Dressing Station and shot a number of the wounded before being driven out. Otherwise the main fighting was on the hillocks, where the tanks were a godsend. We were also wearing down the enemy because of their lack of supplies, and their fire-power was gradually dwindling. It became clear after the first few days that we would win, especially as another division was coming down from the north to support us. By the time they arrived, most of the enemy had abandoned their positions and started their long retreat.

My old unit, 136 Field Regiment, had some casualties, including one young officer wounded and the Second in Command killed. Following a belief that two successive shells never fall in the same place, he had stepped into the crater that a shell had made moments before; but the next shell did fall in exactly the same place. His successor was a courtly man, and the Colonel a bit of a martinet. They became known, after the popular play and movie, as Arsenic and Old Lace.

Our Turn to Chase

After the Japanese retreated, we recovered many of the belongings we had left behind. Presumably the Japanese did not want to carry an ounce more than they had to. For me the most precious item was a Missal given me by my uncle, Ernest Barker, with a clever Latin inscription, which did not appeal to the Japanese. The Missal was blood-stained, and still is.

The siege lasted about 3½ weeks, but time was on our side. We were being supplied by air, but the Japanese were at the end of a very long line of communication and had no air support, and no air reconnaissance. They were short of ammunition, and lethally short of food and medicine. During the siege probably, and on their retreat certainly, more died from disease and starvation than from our shells or bullets.

This siege was our first experience of our troops in sustained battle. Of our British battalions two were excellent and one good. Our Gurkhas were wonderful. Of the ten tribes of Nepal only two are warriors. They are fearless, warlike, disciplined, and of them the Japanese were truly afraid. Our Sikh battalion was ferocious, and the other battalions all acquitted themselves well. So did our services, artillery, signals, Ordnance, supplies, et al.

Like most British soldiers, I have special affection for the Gurkhas. It is said that a Gurkha battalion was converted into paratroops. After due training, they were taken up to 400 feet for their first jump. They were told to jump, and all did except one. They went round again, the officer gave the order again, and the Gurkha refused again. Now, it is unheard of for a Gurkha to disobey an order. At length the Gurkha said,' Sir, come down to 200 feet and I will jump'. 'But then your parachute would not have time to open.' 'Oh' said the Gurkha, 'Do we have parachutes'?

Since WWII, I have read books about the war. It is sad how often the top brass disliked, mistrusted, or were jealous of one another and acted on these feelings. We were greatly blessed at this time and for most of the war that our chain of command, from Bill Slim downwards, got on well and trusted one another and also Mr. Churchill. Elsewhere it was often quite different. Think only of General 'Vinegar Joe' Stilwell's attitude towards Lord Louis Mountbatten or General Chiang Kai-shek. On the brighter side there is a story that Slim was summoned back to London to report to Mr. Churchill. They had some sherry, and then wines with the lunch, followed by brandy and a cigar. The report was yet to be given, so when Churchill offered Slim more brandy and another cigar, he refrained. Churchill's reaction was, 'What's the matter with you, General? You don't drink and you don't smoke'.

After the Japanese had fled, we lingered in the Arakan for several weeks, in the course of which I was present at a picnic on top of the Maungdaw-Buthidaung tunnels with at least two and possibly five generals. When we were relieved, we were sent north-east on a very circuitous journey of around a thousand miles by road to Kohima in the mountains. The roads were narrow, and sometimes had only a central strip of tarmac just one truck wide. That made meeting or passing other vehicles precarious. The last part of our journey was on twisting mountain roads.

At Kohima the Japanese had penetrated 30 miles or so into India's Nagaland. There a ferocious hand-to-hand battle was taking place, comparable in intensity, but not in scale, with the battle of Monte Cassino.

We joined the tail-end of the battle. The area that had been densely wooded was now barren with only a tree trunk or two standing. The Japanese were in strong, well-sited bunkers, each with a narrow slit to fire through. Shells and bombs had to be direct hits on the slit to destroy the bunker. The only other way was by Bangalore torpedo or a flame-thrower. The torpedo was an explosive charge on the end of a pole. Some brave man had to climb on top of the bunker and thrust the pole inside. As each bunker was covered by fire from another bunker, this could be done only at night, and even then only at great risk. With help from our artillery, our infantry succeeded in the end in driving out all the enemy.

At the same time, the Japanese were trying to capture Imphal, a large supply base with airstrips, about 50 miles south-west of Kohima. There too they failed. These three battles, the Arakan, Kohima, and Imphal, the first serious reverses for the Japanese, were the turning points of our Burma campaign. They were not the end of fierce fighting, but from then on the odds were clearly on us. We advanced south, pushing the Japanese before us.

There was a scene during our advance from which I learnt much. We were due to attack a mountainside held by the enemy. Around 10 p.m. General Messervy summoned Brigadier Tim Hely, our head gunner, and ordered him to neutralize the mountain. Tim said the guns of the divisional artillery could not do that.

'Then you must get some guns from XV Corps'.

'Even then it cannot be done. There is no way we can guarantee there will be no Japanese return fire.'

'It must be done.'

'It can't be done.'

This exchange went on for several minutes, louder each time. Both men became quite angry. Eventually the General said, 'It has got to be done, Tim. Now, get out of my tent, you bad-tempered Irishman.'

Tim saluted smartly, turned on his heel and, saying 'It can't be done', walked out into the darkness. Next morning when I came to breakfast, the General was alone in the 'Mess' (some chairs and a table with a tarpaulin stretched above) and in came Tim. I groaned to myself, thinking it would all start up again. What actually happened was that the General asked Tim if he had slept well, Tim answered, 'Yes, Sir, thank you; I slept very well.' They then talked of other things. I have often tried to emulate that 'no rancour', sometimes with success.

About this time I was given four weeks leave. A fellow officer and I went off together to Kashmir, a journey of five or six days, first by road and rail, then by steamer across the River Brahmaputra, then by rail, following the Grand Trunk Road, which runs for 1600 miles from Chittagong to Kabul in Afghanistan, then by road again, and finally on foot. The River Brahmaputra, the least well known of the world's great rivers, is fed by Himalayan snow and is capable of 8 knots. It is 1800 miles long, has an average depth of 124 feet and a maximum of 380 feet. Its discharge in flood, on Google's authority, can be over 3½ million cubic feet per second. We had, with two other officers, our own compartment, whose air conditioning was provided by an enormous block of ice over which a fan played. It made us cooler but not cool.

The Long Pursuit to Rangoon

At Lahore, officials tried to extort a surcharge. I knew that the head of the railway had his office at Lahore, and demanded to see him. Suddenly the officials were all charm. The head happened to be the father of my fellow officer who owned Bulldog Simon. We went on to Rawalpindi by train, and from there took a taxi to Gulmarg in Kashmir, driving through the formidable foothills of the Himalayas, with Nanga Parbat (26,660 feet) visible in the distance. This drive by itself was worth the trip.

Gulmarg is nearly 9000 feet above sea level. We trudged the last thousand feet upward on foot, with our baggage on mules. When we reached our hotel, where we had booked, the landlady said in horror, 'Didn't you get my telegram saying I had no vacancy?' She also thought there was only one of us, having read the signature Captains Henderson and Horner as hyphenated Captain Henderson-Horner. We rolled out our sleeping bags on the floor for the first two nights, and then she found us beds.

We played some golf, sat or walked enjoying the scenery, and on one day rode on horseback to above the tree line, over 16,000 feet. One lady in the party was having difficulty with her horse, and I rode it down. The horse and I, both having red hair, got on well. Much more dangerous was a resident of Gulmarg who was known as the Charpoy Cobra. ("Charpoy" is Urdu for bed.) Innocent subalterns were her prey. Our leave came to an end and after an uneventful journey back, we found our Division well south of where we had left them.

Our next major task was the crossing of the Irrawaddy, 1348 miles long and over a mile wide at the place where we were to cross in February, 1945. Our success was due largely to surprise. We developed a massive operation order, to which my contribution was the traffic plan for all our various units. This was important, as much of the movement was to be at night. As far as I know it worked well. We advanced for the last hundred miles under strict radio silence, and sent out small parties to simulate crossings above and below the real point, which was near Pagan. We were helped also by the absence of Japanese reconnaissance by air. As a result, the bank opposite us was thinly defended, partly by the renegade INA (Indian National Army), whose heart was not in it and who surrendered almost at once.

Even so, it was nearly a disaster. Our first wave rowed silently across in the dark, and established a footing; those who were to follow in boats with outboard motors had not been able to test the motors, since the noise would have destroyed the surprise. Large numbers of the motors either failed to start at all, or took the boats out into midstream, and then failed, leaving the occupants drifting helplessly downstream. As the day wore on, we retrieved the situation, and achieved our task of seizing and holding a bridgehead, through which 17th Indian Division could pass and go on to seize Meiktila, a rail and road junction vital to the enemy. Providentially, the boundary between two Japanese armies bisected their front opposing us, so it took unduly long for information from one half of their front to be relayed to the other. This was the longest opposed river crossing of the war.

We established and enlarged our bridgehead, and the Engineers built a pontoon bridge across the Irrawaddy, quite an achievement over such a broad and fast-flowing river. But it could take only one lane of traffic, and so there were very long waits. A chaplain was needed for a burial on the far side from us. I asked the Royal Air Force (RAF) for a light plane to take him across. 'Don't you know there's a war on'? was the reply. I then called the USAAF. Their reply was 'Sure, and would you like one for each of the burial party'? The USAAF had many more planes there than the RAF, but there was a difference of attitude too.

We stayed at the bridgehead for a while, and had time for some sightseeing at Pagan, the old capital of Burma, where there are some two thousand wats (temples) and stupas (monuments), mostly in ruins, but even the ruins were impressive.

I also had my first flight in an airplane, an L5. This was a single-engine, high-wing monoplane seating a pilot and, behind him, a passenger. I watched the pilot carefully and concluded that in an emergency I could probably land the plane and possibly even take off again. My first amazement was at seeing trees from the top down rather than from the bottom up. On one flight we were over enemy territory and saw an enemy position on a hilltop. The pilot asked if I would like to have a closer look. He said it would be quite safe, as the Japanese had been told that they had command of the air, and so any plane they saw would be friendly. I believed him, and we came down to a few hundred feet. I had one hand-grenade with me, removed the pin, and threw it at the enemy. Our speed was about 90 mph. We had a closer look all right, but I was itching to get out of rifle range.

In due course we left our bridgehead. Soon after, I was promoted to GSO 11 with the rank of Major and became a field officer. That would have been significant in peacetime but made little difference in war, except for the pay.

One evening, our liquor ration for the month – three bottles of beer and a half-bottle of whisky or gin – had just arrived, and I was enjoying some of it after dinner. I found myself alone with a gentle-faced, white-bearded man. I offered him a drink, and to my surprise he accepted. I asked him why he had come and, again to my surprise, he said he had come to conduct a short course in the use of small arms from pistols up to Tommy guns.

He went on to tell me his background. He was a London police officer who had been seconded to the FBI to learn how to deal with gangsters. He was actively present at the death of Dillinger in July 1934. He had then been sent to Palestine to train the police there to deal with the Stern Gang and such. When the Commandos were formed he was brought in to train them. In particular he had to train one man who was to be given two revolvers, 12 bullets in all, and landed by submarine on the north coast of France. There he was to ambush a German Headquarters in an inn where they went each evening to relax. He was to kill all ten of them. He was successful. I asked our visitor what instructions he gave. He said many things, among them that when the commando walked into their room at the inn, he should at once move away from the door to avoid being framed by it. He would have about ten seconds before most of the Germans realized what was happening. If anyone put up his hands, he should shoot him straight away. He had realized what was happening, and so was dangerous. There was much more.

About ten of us signed up for the course. At the end, we were to give a demonstration for our Division's Top Brass. I was to put two shots into a playing card 90 feet away which I did. He was a most gifted instructor.

Years later I was reading *To War with Whitaker* by Lady Ranfurly. She was in Cairo and planning to join her husband in Palestine, when she met a man who advised her to buy a revolver; he would teach her to use it. His technique sounded familiar, so I wrote to her saying so, and added that I had been at school with a number of her Scottish friends. I received a most gracious reply: her instructor and mine were indeed the same.

From Pagan, we turned south down the left bank of the Irrawaddy, through the disabled oilfields of Yenangyaung, past Prome and nearly to Rangoon, where we doubled back northwards and ended in Pegu. All that took months because the Japanese were still fighting vigorous rearguard actions.

During that time, I was sent on a short CW course in Shillong, back in Assam. The topics were Chemical Warfare and Camouflage. As there had been no use of gas and as they did not say much new about camouflage, it was nearly the same as leave. At the end of the course, two of us were asked to design a short exercise to illustrate the lessons of the course. As my partner was an engineer and as part of the exercise involved thunderflashes, a kind of firework to simulate gunfire, I asked my engineer partner to deal with them. Come the day, he lit his thunderflash but held it too long, and it blew off several of his fingers. We both received a grade of D (Distinguished) for the course. He earned it.

When I returned to our division, it was, for the first time, in reserve. The forward troops were being supplied by air, so several of us volunteered to help with the dropping. On the outward flight, I was up in the cockpit with the pilot. We came to a T formation of Valleys. We were flying up the stem of the T with a large, well-wooded mountain blocking our path. I assumed the pilot would turn right or left but he kept straight on. At the last moment he pulled back the joystick and we started to climb. He misjudged the angle and we only just made it over the mountain. The underside of the plane brushed the trees growing on the top of the mountain. That would have been an ignominious death. The drop itself was mostly easy, but the last items were rough gunnysacks of 100 pounds of grain for free dropping without parachutes. We all had bleeding fingertips at the end. Coming back, the pilot played no tricks.

The air was not the only danger: on the ground I walked into a slit trench and badly sprained my ankle. They offered me evacuation, but knowing the horrors of the lines of communication I refused. That may have led to troubles that I had with that ankle later on, but I doubt if the army would recognize any responsibility.

Prome too was on our way. Nearby was a statue of Buddha eighty foot tall. It was free standing, but immediately in front of it was a high earthen mound that we had to climb. When we reached the top, we were about level with the Buddha's mouth and only a few feet from it. It was overwhelming at first but became serenely impressive.

On May 8, 1945, VE (Victory in Europe) Day, the Chief of the Imperial General Staff in London wrote in his diary, 'Thank God the war is over.' No wonder our Fourteenth Army was called the forgotten army. We still had months of war, and but for the atomic bomb, might have had years.

As we approached Pegu, I was sent ahead for the second time to layout Divisional HQ. The area chosen was clay and the monsoon was due. I asked the Engineers for advice, and they recommended digging trenches along the sides of any road that was to be used by vehicles. Would they dig the trenches? No, that was not their job. We dug the trenches, but I sent a skeptical signal back to the General. The rains came and the vehicles too. There were skids and chaos. Had the Japanese had any bombers, there would also have been great slaughter. The slaughter that did take place was of exhausted and often starving Japanese. They were in the hills west of us; we were to their east, blocking their escape route. They could escape only at night. We set in place searchlights and machine guns. Some Japanese did escape each night, but in the mornings it took bulldozers to make trenches for the burial of the bodies. The end came only after the two atomic bombs had been dropped on August 6 and 9. The armistice was signed on August 15, 1945.

Near Pegu there is one of the biggest lying Buddhas, 180 feet long. His ears alone were, symbolically, 20 feet long. He has since been gaudily repainted but was more attractive before. We also saw the gilded

Shwedagon Pagoda in Rangoon. It is 325 feet high and now has 7.1 tonnes of gold coating, about the weight of an elephant. There are about 5500 diamonds in its crown, including one of 76 carats (a little over half an ounce), and over 2300 rubies. It is a center of pilgrimage. The pagoda/stupa and its surroundings were not at their best at the end of the war, but were still magnificent, beautiful, and prayerful.

The Shwedagon Pagoda in Rangoon: Legend has it built in 588 BC, but archaeologists place it between the 6th and 10th centuries AD. It has been remodeled several times. It is a center of pilgrimage.

We Occupy Thailand

After the armistice, several of us were given leave. In a jeep, the Colonel of Signals and I drove over 400 miles on poor roads to Maymyo in the mountains north-east of Mandalay. The site of Mandalay is majestic, but it too had suffered from the war. After a few restful days in Maymyo, we were about to leave for Mogok to see the ruby mines and buy some rubies. As I had only £40 with me I would hardly have made my fortune, but about twenty minutes before we were to set off a signal came that all leave was cancelled and we should return to base at once. That also saved us from the perils of entrusting our jeep to several swinging, bamboo bridges.

We were to go to Bangkok, the capital of what was, for a few days after our arrival, still Siam, but soon became Thailand, or Land of the Free. Before leaving I had two interesting jeep-rides, one with General Evans, who had taken over from General Messervy, the other with Brigadier Hely. They both asked me the same question: 'Now that the war is over, Michael, what are you going to do?' To both I replied that I did not know, but that I had made one decision. To the General the decision was that I was not going to stay in the army. He replied quite seriously, 'But why not? You play cricket; you would do very well in the army.' To the Brigadier, who knew me much better, the decision was that I wanted to do something that I wanted to do 24 hours a day, and not something that I did from 9 to 5, so that for the rest of the time I could do what I wanted to do. He said nothing. When I became a monk, I wrote to tell him. In his reply he reminded me of this conversation and said that he knew then what I was going to do. Remarkably perspicacious, considering that I myself did not know.

I heard no qualms expressed at that time about the atomic bombs, of which we admittedly knew very little. Rather, we all sighed sighs of relief at the armistice, which saved us months, perhaps years, of fighting. We did think that our days of fatigue and danger were over, but they were not. I had less sleep in our first few days in Bangkok than at any other time in the war, and the dangers were different but not fewer.

Some sixteen of us took off from Rangoon in the leading plane to

Don Muang, the airport for Bangkok, armed to the teeth with a revolver apiece, to meet 16,000 Japanese who might or might not know of the armistice. Our first danger was from black, torpedo-shaped clouds with interior currents that sometimes devoured planes. We dived down to the sea until we were almost surfing. Then over the mountains which lay between Rangoon and Bangkok, we met a storm fierce enough for the plane after us, which carried all our files, to have to jettison most of them. It was odd how seldom in Thailand we missed those files.

We landed safely and were welcomed by the Japanese, taken to their Officers' Mess, and offered a drink, which, after that flight, was just what we needed. But the General wisely ordered 'No Fraternization'. So we were taken to an enormous, empty hangar, which would be ours for as long as we wanted.

As evening came, the hangar grew darker and we unpacked our various oil- and Coleman-lamps. We had been without electricity for nearly two years, so this came naturally. Then I saw a row of light switches on the wall of the hangar and hesitated. Might they be booby-trapped? I switched on as many as I could together. That blaze of light is something I remember still.

After a few days, three elderly but shiny Rolls Royces transported us to a palace in downtown Bangkok. 'Why three?' we asked. 'You'll see' they replied. After a few miles, one overheated and we transferred to the second; after a few more miles, the second overheated. The third got us to our palace, one of many. There were many because one previous king may have had as many as 82 children. They were all royal, and needed palaces, but there were several grades of royalty, and each generation of children went down a grade, until they ended as commoners.

I was on the fifth floor of our palace, with a beautiful marble bath, a six foot cube, with steps down into it, but no running water. My batman and I agreed that we must have at least one token bath in it. He brought up enough warm water to cover the floor of the bath. I dipped into it, and said he could do the same. I do not know whether he did. It was also good to sleep in a bed again.

The Siamese had on the whole cooperated with the Japanese during the war, and so were very anxious now to show us they had acted under duress, as for the most part they had; so they were most hospitable, made us members of clubs, and so on. We got to know one family, whose head had been Prime Minister. He was sent to Australia with a large sum to buy racehorses for the royal stable. He used the money for a series of parties 'to put Thailand on the map'. He then wired back to Bangkok for some money to buy horses. He was recalled in disgrace. To restore the family fortune, he and his two beautiful daughters started a circus, to which we were invited. I remember only the Thai boxing, which was much more acrobatic than our boxing.

We had a daily staff meeting of all the Top Brass. A river flows through Bangkok. At that time there was only one bridge over it, and that bridge had been bombed by the allies. Our general, indicating very firmly the urgency of the matter, asked the head Engineer (CRE) whether and when it would be safe for traffic. He said that he wanted an answer at tomorrow's meeting. On the morrow, the CRE reported that there was a much better site for a bridge about a mile upstream. Asked how long it would take to build the bridge and the necessary access roads, he replied that it would take six months to a year. The general nearly exploded in apoplexy. Fortunately for the CRE, further survey showed that the bridge was safe to use. Experts can be wonderful in their field of expertise, but can still miss the point in the wider context.

There was also a daily meeting with the Japanese liaison officer (LO), at which he told us what they had been doing and what their plans and needs were. Our main job was to help them get back to Japan. We met in the morning, but once we summoned him late in the evening. He arrived having clearly consumed too much saké. He denied this, so our colonel drew a chalk line on the floor and asked him to walk along it. Instead, he charged down the line and knocked our colonel off his balance with a sharp blow of his own head to the colonel's stomach. He was disgraced and replaced. Not long after that, our colonel was posted to command his old battalion, and I took his place as GSO 1, the General's chief operations staff officer. There were no military operations, so I was not wholly out of my depth, but the job included dealing with the Japanese LO. There was to be no fraternization, but I did learn quite a lot from him about what the atom bomb had done in Hiroshima.

We were busy, but mostly with unexciting routine work. We had some visitors, including General 'Boy' Browning and General Auchinleck, who was startled that I had never been to a Staff College. But the most interesting were Lord and Lady Mountbatten. We took them to dinner at the Hoi Tien Lao, which served the best Chinese food I have had anywhere, including China; not surprising, since many of the ingredients start in the Gulf of Siam: shark's fin, bird's nest soup, etc. On this occasion we had 100-years-old pigeon's eggs, which are small, hard, and slick. With chopsticks one had to pick up an egg from the bowl, dip it in the sauce, and transfer it to one's mouth. Soon the floor was littered with eggs.

No Longer at War

Just before Christmas, the General told me he was making plans to visit Angkor Wat in Cambodia, a difficult trip to organize in those days. I was thrilled, until he said that he and I could not be away together. That was mildly flattering and deeply disappointing. Instead, when he came back, a friend and I were given leave to spend some days at Hua Hin, which then was the royal summer palace – the king was in exile in Europe – and is now a seaside resort. We played golf. Our forecaddies, until we told them otherwise, thought their job was to move balls from the rough onto the fairway, or from off the green onto the green, and were amazed when we demurred. But the highlight was a five-mile gallop along the firm sand of the sea shore with occasional splashes through little inlets. Horses and riders loved it, but we had to let the horses cool down for a while before going back to the stable.

We also played some cricket. My only white shirt was far too tight across the shoulders, and I bowled as badly as I have ever bowled; I bowled one good ball, which went for an easy catch, and a county cricketer dropped it. I then caught as good a catch as I have ever caught; but my bowling lost us that match.

I acted as GSO 1 for four months and about twenty-eight days, and we normally received the acting rank and pay for any job we did for three months or more. But the army sent my predecessor on leave for a month and took that out of my time, and then sent my successor on leave for a month and took that too out of my time, thus reducing my time on paper to two months and twenty-eight days. I did not mind about the rank, but the pay would have been useful.

Shortly before my successor arrived, we received a signal that there was to be in England a course for field officers on Combined Operations. No one else in the division applied. Though I was more interested in England than in Combined Ops, I did apply and was accepted. Little did I know what I was in for.

The plane left Bangkok for Rangoon and the flight was without storms, but just after landing at Rangoon, we suddenly swerved violently off the runway and then back on again. A truck was coming up the runway towards us and our pilot had somehow to lift one wing and let the truck go under it. He was successful. We flew on to Calcutta and were taken to a transit hotel on the main street, Chowringhee. We were warned that there might be some disturbance, but we had a quiet night. Next day a number of us had to go to convert our travel warrants into tickets for England. A truck took us to the travel agent and we made our conversions. By that time a crowd of several thousand had gathered and was rioting in a main square, which lay across our way back to the hotel. Our experienced driver had everyone get into the back and lie down; I was to sit by him in front. When we reached the square, the crowd was there in a bad mood and with stones in their hands. I looked at the driver; he assured me he knew what to do. He accelerated and headed straight at the crowd. Just before he reached them, he braked violently, the truck reared for a moment onto its two front wheels, the crowd parted, and we raced through the gap. One small stone hit my hand, and even that has made me feel quite differently when I read accounts in the Bible and elsewhere of people being stoned. The rioters were seeking independence from the British Empire. Back at our hotel, we were advised not to go out, but to be ready to leave at any time. The crowds were burning cars all the way down Chowringhee.

At 2 a.m. our call came and we were driven to a seaplane waiting for us on Calcutta's Hooghly River. I had never flown in a seaplane before, so this was an added and pleasant excitement. Take-off was very smooth; we stopped at various lakes en route, and arrived at Karachi safely. When we landed, or should one say 'watered', the bow wave past our windows was a beautiful, foamy curve. No sooner had we disembarked than I saw a four-engine monster land and heard it then accelerate with a great roar. I feared the worst, but I was simply hearing for the first time reversible-pitch propellers.

We transferred to a Liberator for the trip to Lydda, in what was still Palestine. Our plane happened to have a small hole in the fuselage just over my head. I thought this might be welcome air-conditioning, but when we reached 10,000 feet, the air was bitterly cold. The plane was crowded, so I could not move. When we reached Lydda, I went to the transit office and found there were no seats on any plane going to

England. I was expostulating in the outer office when the door of the inner office opened and out came John Wilkes, who had been an officer in 136 Field Regiment with me. He recognized my voice and came to my rescue. There was a group of RAF other ranks who needed a draft conducting officer to take them to England. If I was willing to sign in as Squadron-Leader Horner, I could conduct them. I signed in, and next morning we took off. Our route was to be across the south-eastern corner of the Mediterranean, along the coast of North Africa, and back across the Mediterranean to Catania in Sicily for the night. Our DC 3, or Dakota, was to stop in North Africa to refuel.

But the North African coast was covered in fog. At Sidi Barrani they sent us on to Tobruk, and at Tobruk on to Benghazi. By then we were almost out of fuel, so Benghazi told us to land on a disused strip in the desert, and they would send us a truck with fuel for the plane and food for us. They did this. Meanwhile the pilot had paced the strip and found it was 397 yards long. With full tanks and a full load of passengers he needed 750 yards to take off. In addition, there were telephone wires at the end of the strip. What should he do? We decided we could hardly stay the night, so there was only one choice. He took the plane back right to the end of the strip, revved up like mad and careered down the strip. We were airborne, and so were the telephone wires, which we hoped were as disused as the strip; we made it to Catania.

Catania is close to Mount Etna (11,000 feet). Next day, when we took off just after dawn, the cloud base was about halfway up Etna. We climbed up through the clouds and above them the sun was tingeing the white clouds with pink, and the top half of Etna was sitting on the clouds. That was a sight to remember.

We landed in the south-west of England, were taken by coach up to London, and I then had to travel back to the south-west to join the course a day late. Our instructor thought Bangkok was the capital of Vietnam, but he was much better on Combined Ops. I had some leave after the course and then flew back to 7th Indian Division, which by then had moved from Thailand to Ipoh in Northern Malaya. The flight back was dull by comparison. Our pilot kindly circled the pyramids and the Sphinx; we were delayed in Sri Lanka; we landed in Singapore. I then took the train almost the whole length of Malaya to Ipoh.

I was looking forward to rejoining old friends, but almost all of them had left. There was a new general, who was reported, falsely I hope, to have said, 'Thank God the war is over, and we can get back to real soldiering'. But there was that kind of atmosphere around. I did my job, kept my head down and longed for demobilization.

There were bright spots. I met Ian Stemson, a brilliant tennis player, who became a lifelong friend, and we had a remarkable dinner. The dinner was at a restaurant across a range of hills from Ipoh. We ordered ahead, but as the order had to pass through five languages, I was dubious about our getting what we wanted. Our party drove over the hills in two jeeps, and we did get what we wanted. After dinner we all drove back. We did not decide to race, but each jeep wanted to be home before the other. At one point on the winding road, one of our headlights started to flicker. Ian and I did not want to stop, so I clambered out onto the hood and fixed the flickering light– yet another post-war near death experience. Ian later married a wife from Chicago, which in due course brought him to visit her family, and so to visit me en route.

At last the orders for demobilization for both of us came through together. Ian and I drove the length of Malaya to Singapore to meet our ship. We stopped in Kuala Lumpur with some Chinese friends of his. The daughter of the house wore wooden clogs, which played two different notes on the stone floor of the courtyard. After school she took out her paper, ink and brush and started her homework at the top right hand corner of the page, finished that column and moved to the left for the next column. It was real calligraphy. We were just finishing their dinner of ten courses or so, when the phone rang. It was another of Ian's Chinese friends asking if we had forgotten that they had invited us to dinner. We ate at least twenty courses.

We reached Singapore and settled in at the transit camp. We had a week or two to wait for our ship. Singapore had at that time the dirtiest waterfront I have seen, but it is now beautifully clean. There was an enormous outdoor swimming pool, where the water temperature was in the 80°s F just from the sun. We made a brief excursion up the attractive East coast, found a more or less abandoned hotel (but it did have a caretaker) and spent the night there. There was a beautiful, sandy beach, a full moon, a warm sea, and no jellyfish. Next morning, we thanked the caretaker, to which he replied, 'Please do not say anything about it'. We thought we might be getting him into trouble, but it was merely his version of the common English reply of the time 'Don't mention it'.

We had an uneventful journey home through the Suez Canal. What I would do after the war was naturally very much in my prayers and on my mind. Usually when faced with major decisions, it is not so much that I suddenly make the decision. Rather, I come to recognize that I have made the decision. So it was this time. One evening somewhere in the middle of the Indian Ocean I recognized that I had decided to ask the Abbot of Ampleforth that I might join his monastery. Nothing dramatic occurred, no voices, no visions, but the call was quite clear.

The Mediterranean was almost startlingly blue, but when we passed Gibraltar, the weather became more and more gray and damp. We reached Liverpool in steady rain. Nor was our welcome by Customs much brighter. I was standing in the queue behind a young lady, whom I had never seen before. We were talking, and she said she had been with ENSA (Entertainments National Service Association) providing entertainment for the troops abroad. The Customs official started giving her a bad time and I said something in her defense. He then turned on me and said I was her husband and part of ENSA. I said I did not have either honor. I was not in uniform, so I went and changed and chose another official. I heard later that one of the passengers claimed to have 'forgotten' that he had 750 pairs of silk stockings in his trunk – and this at a time when silk stockings in England were rare and almost priceless – so perhaps the official had some excuse for being grumpy. We were then given a suit, a ticket to our home and, I think, some pocket money, and then we were free.

After Demobilization

All that remained was to write to the Abbot of Ampleforth, and then tell my family the result. My mother reacted with a mixture of joy and sorrow, my father with incomprehension and disappointment, and my uncle David with congratulations. He was the only Catholic on my father's side of the family. There were also the three Horner aunts, my great aunts, who lived to be 99, 99, and 92. They asked me what I was planning to do now. I said I was going to be a monk at Ampleforth, and waited for the disapproval that I expected. Aunt Muriel said instead, 'A month, dear? That's a very long time to spend there.' I tried again with 'priest', to which she replied, 'That's good, there has always been a priest in the family.' She was referring to the Horners' advowson, or Right of Presentation of a Priest to the Parish, in this case to the Church of England Parish of Mells in Somerset.

And so my war ended, neither with a bang, nor with a whimper.

There were some loose ends. I was awarded an MBE, and twice 'Mentioned in Despatches'. I could not attend the award of the MBE, normally by Her Majesty, as I was by then in the novitiate at Ampleforth.

At the first meeting of the 7th Indian Division Officers' Dining Club, General Evans approached one of my friends with 'Have you heard about poor Michael? They have locked him up.' My friends thought I had perpetrated some fell deed.

While I was still at Ampleforth, General Evans was appointed GOC-in-C of Northern Command and was stationed in York. He once inspected Ampleforth's OTC; he also came to watch several of our cricket matches – he had opened the batting for the Warwickshire Regiment with Lieutenant, later Field Marshal, Bernard Montgomery. He used to greet me warmly, and my monastic stock rose accordingly. When I knew I was coming to Saint Louis, I went to his headquarters in York to say goodbye. I asked for him, and his ADC appeared and, on seeing an unknown priest, understandably tried to protect his general. We debated the point for a while and I was about to leave a message, when the General heard my voice and came out to resolve the standoff. He then very kindly invited me to lunch at his home, and we had a very friendly farewell.

Years later in Saint Louis, I was talking to one of our teachers, who had been a regular officer in the Royal Navy. He asked if I was receiving a pension. I had forgotten all about WWII pensions. They start when you are 65, and you must apply before you are 70. As I was in between, I wrote to those concerned, and the reply stated that the deductions from my pay fell £200 short of the minimum. I asked what would happen if I sent them £200 now. They said I would get a pension. I sent the money and they sent me the due instalment of my pension, and they still do.

The most heart-warming event was that when, in 1953, I was ordained priest at Ampleforth, all the four men of the Artillery Headquarters of which I was briefly a member came to the Ordination, and only two were Catholic. The night before the Ordination, they met at the Station Hotel in York and held in its rather staid foyer a rehearsal of how to meet the Abbot on the following day. Bulgy Leach, sitting in an armchair, took the part of the Abbot, and had the others come to him, genuflect, kiss his imaginary ring, and greet him as "Father Abbot'.